Printed By Createspace, An Amazon.com Company

By Christian Kid Notebook

Made in the USA
Coppell, TX
28 January 2022

72478625R00075